The M

Contents

written by Barry Holden

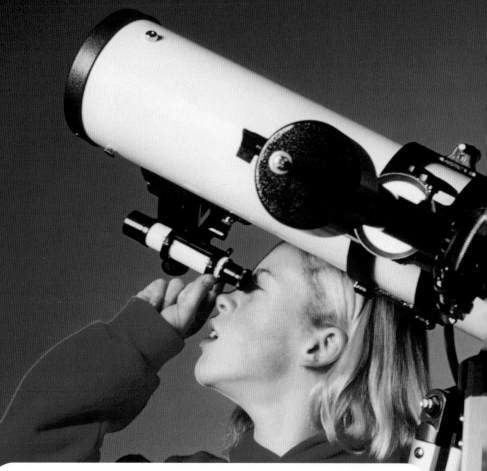

Look at all the stars in the sky at night. They are a long way out in Space. The stars are so far away that they look very small.

telescope

We can't see them in the daytime, but we know that they are up there.

We live on the planet called
Earth. Our part of Space is
called the Milky Way.

Milky Way

Most of the things we can see in the sky are in the Milky Way.

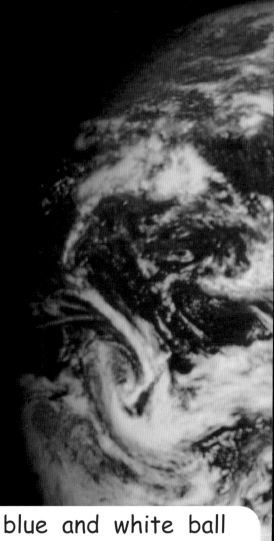

Earth looks like a blue and white ball when it is seen from Space. It is smaller than any of the stars. Earth is the only planet that has water, and we all need water to live.

Earth turns as it goes around the Sun. It takes a day for one turn, and a year to go right around the Sun.

Did you know that the Sun is a very big star? It is more than a hundred times bigger than Earth! The Sun is the closest star to Earth.

sun

As Earth turns to the Sun, our day gets light and warm. When Earth turns away, it gets dark, and we can get very cold.

Our Moon is much smaller than Earth.
It goes slowly around us, and it takes
a month to go right around.

The Moon is round, but sometimes we can only see part of it.

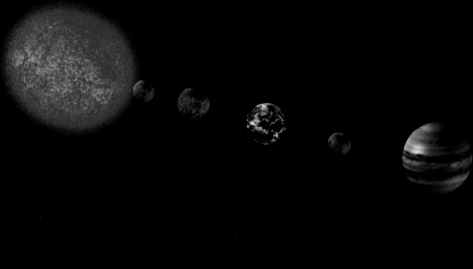

Do you know the names of 8 planets in our Space? They all go around the Sun. Can you see which one is Earth? It is the third planet away from the Sun.

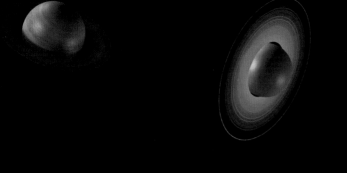

The planet called Jupiter is the biggest one, but it is much smaller than the Sun.

There are lots and lots more stars out in Space. They are a long way past our Milky Way. They are so far away that our eyes can't see them.

observatory

We can only see some of them if we look through a very big telescope.

astronaut

Astronauts go out to explore Space.
Men have been walking on the Moon!
Where will they go next?